D0130943

ROMÂNIA

a photographic memoir · *eine fotografische Erinnerung*

Photos / *Fotos*
© Florin Andreescu

Text / *Text*
Mariana Pascaru

Traducere engleză / *English translation*
Alistair Blyth

Traducere germană / *Deutsche Übersetzung*
Lia Gross-Marcu
Grete Klaster-Ungureanu

Image processing / *Layout*
Gina Büll

Descriere CIP a Bibliotecii Naționale
ANDREESCU, FLORIN
    România: a photographic memoir = eine fotografische Erinnerung
foto: Florin Andreescu; text: Mariana Pascaru; trad. engleză: Alistair Blyth,
trad. germană: Lia Gross Marcu & Grete Klaster-Ungureanu.
București : AD LIBRI, 2006
    ISBN (10) 973-7887-14-X; ISBN (13) 978-973-7887-14-6

913(498)(084)

Editat © AD LIBRI srl
tel/fax:01-212.35.67, 610.37.92; e-mail: adlibri@b.astral.ro; www.adlibri.ro

Toate drepturile asupra prezentei lucrări aparțin editurii **Ad Libri.**
Reproducerea integrală sau parțială a textelor sau ilustrațiilor
este posibilă numai cu acordul prealabil scris al editurii **Ad Libri.**

First cover: Children in traditional costumes, Turț village, Țara Oașului
Umschlagbilder: Kinder in der traditionellen Tracht des Dorfes Turț, Oașer Land.

ROMÂNIA

a photographic memoir • *eine fotografische Erinnerung*

Photos / *Fotos*: Florin Andreescu

Text / *Text*: Mariana Pascaru

All places have their own particular way of surprising the traveller. A fulfilling journey sometimes depends on the apparently minor details – on the harmonious rather than the spectacular aspect of a landscape; on the serenity rather than the splendour that envelops one of the world's hidden corners, discovered by chance; on the gentle charm of the provincial settlement rather than the stifling monumentality of the conurbation. At the core of our memories, we rediscover the tranquillity that enveloped us when we arrived in places just as pure and wild as on the first day of creation, the warmth of locals always ready to tell of legends, the savour of unique traditional recipes, the picturesque ancestral customs. It is from the accumulation of these and other similar impressions that the pure essences of an unforgettable journey are distilled.

This album might be regarded as the "chronicle" of such a journey: it does not attempt to convince you that Romania is the "paradise" of the Balkans, but merely to show you that, to the attentive eye, shards of ineffable beauty reveal themselves here. If you are travelling to Romania for the first time, you will do well to give up any kind of preconception and prepare yourself for surprises, discovering wonders you will never have anticipated.

Romania is that place where the *Danubius* (or Danube), the sacred river of ancient times, finishes its journey, emptying into the Black Sea after traversing 1,075 kilometres of Romanian territory. The Roman legions once crossed the Danube on their way to Dacia, the realm of the "immortal" Getes, or Dacians - the ancestors of the modern Romanians - who worshipped Zalmoxis. After the Romans defeated the Dacians, the south of this territory became a Roman province, named *Dacia Felix* (in other words, "Fruitful Dacia"). The ethnic mix of Dacians and Romans provided the basis for the emergence of the Romanian people, which has been called "an island of Latinity in a Slavic sea". It is to be wondered just how it was possible for a language of Latin origin, like Italian, Spanish or French, to flourish in a part of Europe that has been reckoned the domain of the Slavic languages par excellence.

Any journey through these regions will reveal to you continually different facets of Romania, almost as if its metamorphoses were inexhaustible. A Romania with the perfume of the Levant; a Romania that preserves the memory of the "little Paris" epoch; a Romania of churches; a sub-Mediterranean Romania, in the vicinity of the Danube; and a Romania of Carpathian mountain peaks are just some of the facets that this astonishing land is waiting to reveal to you.

Today, as Europe transforms itself and searches for a new identity, a journey through Romania yields us significant revelations. Beyond the hesitations that accompany adoption of the norms for harmonisation imposed by the EU, we shall discover in Romania a land that has always been conscious of its European identity and is endowed with a culture undeniably rooted in European values.

*J*eder Ort überrascht den Reisenden in seiner Art. Der Erfolg der Reise hängt manchmal von scheinbar unwichtigen Kleinigkeiten ab - von der Harmonie der Landschaft vielleicht mehr als von ihrer Großartigkeit; von der Heiterkeit und Ruhe, die ein durch Zufall entdeckter verborgener Winkel ausstrahlt, eher als von seinem Glanz; vom lieblichen Zauber der ländlichen Ortschaften und nicht von der erdrückenden Monumentalität der städtischen Ballungszentren. Unser Erinnerungsvermögen lässt uns die Ruhe wiederfinden, die uns umgab, als wir an Stätten weilten, die so unberührt und wildromantisch waren wie am ersten Tag der Schöpfung; die Wärme der Einheimischen, die immer gerne bereit sind, Altüberliefertes zu erzähen; den würzigen Geschmack traditioneller Speisen, einzig in ihrer Art; das Malerische uralter Bräuche. Aus solcherart gesammelten Eindrücken ergeben sich schließlich die bleibenden Erinnerungen an eine unvergessliche Reise.

Dieses Album kann als "Chronik" einer solchen Reise gelten. Es will Sie nicht zu überzeugen versuchen, dass Rumänien das "Paradies" des Balkans sei, es will Ihnen nur zeigen, dass ein aufmerksames Auge hier auf Schritt und Tritt ungeahnte Schönheiten entdecken kann. Falls Sie zum ersten Mal durch Rumänien reisen, ist es angebracht, auf jegliche Vorurteile zu verzichten und sich überraschen zu lassen. So werden Sie Wunderdinge erleben, die Sie gar nicht erwartet haben.

Rumänien ist das Land, wo der uralte heilige Strom Danubius (rumänisch: Dunărea - die Donau) den letzten Teil seines Laufes vollbringt; 1075 km lang durchmisst er es bis zu seiner Mündung ins Schwarze Meer.

Die Donau überquerten einst die römischen Truppen auf ihrem Weg nach Dazien, dem Gebiet der "unsterblichen" Geten (oder Dazier) - der Urahnen der Rumänen -, die Zamolxes anbeteten. Nach dem Sieg der Römer über die Dazier wurde der südliche Teil ihres Gebietes zu einer römischen Provinz: Dacia Felix (glückliches Dazien) genannt. Dieses Völkergemisch war die Grundlage, aus der das rumänische Volk hervorging, von dem es heißt, es stelle "eine Oase der Latinität in einem slawischen Meer" dar. In der Tat ist es staunenswert, wie sich eine gleich dem Italienischen, Französischen oder Spanischen aus dem Lateinischen hervorgegangene Sprache in einem Teil Europas hat entwickeln können, der als ausgesprochen slawischer Bereich betrachtet wurde.

Auf jeglicher Reise durch dieses Land werden Sie immer neue Facetten Rumäniens entdecken, als ob seine Metamorphosen unerschöpflich wären. Ein Rumänien von levantinischem Duft, ein Rumänien, das noch an die Zeiten des "kleinen Paris" erinnert, ein Rumänien der Kirchen, ein an der Donau liegendes submediterranes Rumänien, ein Rumänien der Karpatenhöhen. Das sind nur einige wenige Facetten, unter denen sich uns dieses erstaunliche Land darbietet.

Heute, da Europa im Zeichen der Umwandlungen steht und sich auf der Suche nach einer neuen Identität befindet, kann uns eine Reise durch Rumänien zu einigen wichtigen Einsichten verhelfen. Abgesehen von dem Zögern, mit dem die von der EU festgelegten angleichenden Normen angenommen werden, finden Sie hier ein Land vor, das sich seiner Zugehörigkeit zu Europa seit jeher bewusst ist, dessen Kultur den europäischen Werten um nichts nachsteht.

Peaks, stone and water, sun and clouds

1. Giptel, Fels und Wasser, Sonne und Wolken

*I*f you come Romania, you won't have to worry about any lack of things to do; the hardest thing will be to choose one of the countless tourist itineraries available. Although its surface area does not exceed 240,000 square kilometres, Romania can boast almost every form of geographic relief: mountains, sea, delta, lakes, hills, valleys with winding waterways, caves, ravines, cataracts... The imagination of nature seems to have been inexhaustible in these places.

On the mountain paths that criss-cross the Romanian Carpathians, you will discover landscapes to take your breath away. Invigorated by the pure air of the Romanian high places, you will be overwhelmed by "immense forces", as it is aptly put by the Romanians who flock at weekends to the mountain resorts of the Prahova Valley: Sinaia, the former summer residence of the royal family; Bușteni; Azuga; and Predeal. In summer, the mountains are bathed in the scent of the wildflowers that speckle the meadows or cling to the crags; in winter, they are cloaked in dazzling white, and the excellently equipped ski slopes bustle with activity.

The efforts of those who set out to conquer the Romanian Carpathians always reap rich rewards: every ascent becomes a journey of initiation at the end of which the mountain reveals its mysteries. You can choose between the apparently unassailable Făgăraș range, with its Moldoveanu peak (2544 metres); Piatra Craiului (a crest indented with bluish-white limestone, towering cliff faces, rocky shelfs, crags and scree); the "rocky fortresses" of the Apuseni Mountains (the domain of karst phenomena such as the Ponor Forts, the Living Flame Glacier, the Padiș Plateau, the Galbena, the Warm Someș, and the Rămeți gorges); the Retezat Massif, with its eighty glacial tarns (Bucura, Zănoaga, Tăul Negru, Ana, Lia, Viorica), which is home to a 54,400 hectare national park, declared a Biosphere Reservation; the Maramureș Mountains, traversed by the Vaser Valley, along which runs an old narrow-gauge steam railway; the Gutâi,

with its Cockerel Crest, formed of volcanic rocks; the Rodna Mountains, with their numerous glacial features (crests, valleys, moraines); the Rarău Massif, with its bizarre Ladies Rocks; and the volcanically formed Călimani, on whose plateau rise up the twelve Apostles Rocks, which seemingly transport us back to the mythical beginnings of the world.

Nor can we neglect the marvellous hidden face of the mountains of Romania. We refer, of course, to the twelve thousand caves beneath the mountains, whose galleries stretch for more than a thousand kilometres: the Scărișoara Glacier, the Cave of Bears, the Bistrița Cave, the Cave of the Women, the Cave of the Bats, Ialomița Cave, the Cave of Wind, Meziad Cave. The splendours of these "subterranean palaces" seem to have been taken from the world of the Arabian Nights.

The Carpathians have been likened to a "castle of waters", for it is here that hundreds of rivers and streams begin their journey through Romania, representing ninety-eight per cent of the country's network of waters, including the Olt, Mureș, Ialomița, Someș, Argeș, Siret, Jiu, and Rămeț. For the length of the Nera, Turda, Bistrița, Olteț, Runcu (Sohodol), Bicaz, and Tătaru gorges you can witness the millennial, monumental struggle between water and mountain. And these are just a few of the two hundred gorges to be found in Romania.

Romania's 3,500 lakes each reflect their own unique image of the sky. In the glimmer of their waters are gathered the petrified shadows of the mountains, the restlessly changing clouds and the dazzle of the sun, forming surreal vistas, occasionally disturbed by the glint of airborne wings. In Romania, there are to be found volcanic lakes (St Ana), glacial lakes (Bucura, Zănoaga, Gâlcescu, Bâlea), karst lakes (Iezerul Ighiu), saline lakes (Bottomless Lake, Ursu), natural reservoirs (Roșu), and man-made lakes (the Iron Gates, on the Danube; Izvorul Muntelui or Bicaz, on the Bistrița River; Vidraru, on the Argeș; Vidra, on the Lotru; Scropoasa, on the Ialomița).

Wenn Sie in Rumänien ankommen, brauchen Sie sich keine Sorgen zu machen über die Auswahlmöglichkeiten, die Ihnen zur Verfügung stehen. Schwieriger ist es, sich für eine der zahlreichen touristischen Trassen zu entscheiden, die Ihnen hier vorgeschlagen werden. Obwohl Rumänien nur knappe 240 000 qkm misst, findet man hier so gut wie alle Reliefformen: Gebirge, Meer, Delta, Seen, Berge, Hügel, flußbenetzte Täler, Höhlen, Klammen, Engpässe, Wasserfälle...

Entlang der Gebirgspfade, die sich durch die rumänischen Karpaten schlängeln, können Sie atemberaubende Landschaften entdecken. Die herrliche und saubere Gebirgsluft wird Sie trunken machen und "Riesenkräfte" in Ihnen erwecken, wie es die Rumänen behaupten, die am Wochenende die Kurorte des Prahovatales zwischen dem Bucegi-Gebirge und den Baiului-Bergen überfluten: Sinaia, ehemalige Sommerresidenz der königlichen Familie, Bușteni, Azuga, Predeal.

Wer die rumänischen Karpaten erobern will, wird für seine Mühe reichlich belohnt. Jeder Aufstieg ist ein Weg zu neuen Erfahrungen, an dessen Ende einem weitere Geheimnisse des Berges enthüllt werden. Sie können wählen zwischen dem Fogarascher Gebirge (Munții Făgărașului), das schwer zu erobern scheint und dessen höchste Spitze, der Moldoveanu, 2544 m emporragt; dem Königstein (Piatra Craiului) mit seinem gezackten Kamm aus weißgrauem Kalkstein, seinen hohen Wänden, tiefen Schluchten, Felsvorsprüngen und Geröllfeldern; der "steinernen Burg" der Westkarpaten (Munții Apuseni), wo die Karstphänomene zu Hause sind: Cetățile Ponorului, die Eishöhle Focul Viu, das Padiș-Plateau, die Galbenei-Klamm, die Klamm des Warmen Somesch, die Râmeți-Klamm; dem Retezat-Massiv mit seinen 80 Gletscherseen (Bucura, Zănoaga, Tăul Negru, Ana, Lia, Viorica), wo sich auch ein 54 000 Hektar großer Nationalpark befindet, der zum Biosphärenreservat erklärt wurde; den Maramurescher Bergen, vom Wassertal durchzogen, das die alte "Mocănița", eine Schmalspurbahn mit Dampflok,

entlangfährt; dem Gutâi-Gebirge mit seinem "Hahnenkamm" (Creasta Cocoșului) aus vulkanischem Gestein; den Rodna-Bergen mit ihren zahlreichen Spuren aus der Eiszeit (Grate, Täler, Kessel, Moränen); dem Rarău-Massiv mit den bizarren Felsgebilden "Pietrele Doamnei".

Auch die erstaunliche, weniger sichtbare Seite der rumänischen Berge können wir nicht unerwähnt lassen; und zwar beziehen wir uns auf die 12 000 Höhlen in ihrem Untergrund, deren Galerien zusammengenommen 1000 km ausmachen: die Eishöhle Scărișoara, die Bärenhöhle, die Bistrița-Höhle, die Weiberhöhle, die Fledermaushöhle, die Ialomița-Höhle, die Windhöhle, die Meziad-Höhle.

Die Karpaten können mit einem "Wasserturm" verglichen werden, denn von hier beginnen Hunderte von Flüssen und Bächen ihren Lauf durch Rumänien, 98% des hydrographischen Netzes des Landes: Olt, Mureș, Ialomița, Someș, Argeș, Siret, Jiu, Râmeți. In den Klammen der Nera, von Turda, der Bistrița, des Olteț, Runcu (Sohodol), Bicaz, Tătaru können Sie die Geschichte der gewaltigen Kämpfe verfolgen, die diese Gewässer Jahrmillionen lang mit dem Berg führen mussten. Und diese Aufzählung umfasst nur einige von den 200 Klammen, die es auf dem Gebiet Rumäniens gibt.

Die rund 3500 Seen, die man in Rumänien finden kann, sind ebenso viele Spiegelbilder des Himmels. Auf ihrer Oberfläche spiegeln sich die starren Schatten der Berge, die unruhig dahinziehenden Wolken, das Glitzern der Sonnenstrahen - eine surrealistische Landschaft, die ab und zu von darüber hinwegfliegenden Vögeln belebt wird, die sich im Wasser spiegeln. Es gibt hier Seen vulkanischen Ursprungs (der Sankt-Anna-See), Gletscherseen (Bucura, Zănoaga, Gâlcescu, Bâlea), Karstseen (Iezerul Ighiu), Salzseen (Lacul fără fund, Ursu), natürliche Stauseen (Lacul Roșu), antropische Seen (Porțile der Fier - das Eiserne Tor - an der Donau, Izvorul Muntelui oder Bicaz an der Bistrița, Vidraru am Argeș, Vidra am Lotru, Scropoasa an der Ialomița).

The Black Tarn and the Rocky Valley in the Retezat Mountains.
Der See Tăul Negru und das Pietrele-Tal im Retezat-Gebirge.

The matchless colours of the Romanian forest.
Die unvergleichliche Farbenpracht der rumänischen Wälder.

The high altitude Transfăgărășan highway, with a length of ninety kilometres, traverses the Făgăraș Mountains, reaching the shores of the Bâlea Lake (2034 m).
Die Transfogarascher, eine 90 km lange Höhenstraße, die das Fogarascher Gebirge überquert und auch am Rande des 2034 m hoch gelegenen Gletschersees Bâlea vorbeiführt.

◁ View over the Bucegi Mountains and Piatra Craiului.
Blick auf den Königstein (Piatra Craiului) und das Bucegi-Gebirge

The Rucăr-Bran corridor, winter.
Winter im Durchbruch Rucăr-Bran.

The Bukowina region.
Das Gebiet der Bukowina.

Household in the village of Cârlibaba (Suceava county).
Eine Bauernwirtschaft im Dorf Cârlibaba (Kreis Suceava).

The Glacier Caves at Scărişoara and the Living Flame Glacier in the Apuseni Mountains.
Die Eishöhlen Scărişoara und Focul Viu in den Westkarpaten (Munţii Apuseni).

Houses scattered over the hills of the Rucăr-Bran Corridor.
Vereinzelt stehende Häuser auf den Höhen längs des Rucăr-Bran-Durchbruchs.

Whispers, murmers, burbling waters...
Flüsterndes, murmelndes, sprudelndes Wasser . . .

In the Romanian mountains, twilight offers us a veritable feast of colours.
Das Licht der untergehenden Sonne bietet uns in den rumänischen Bergen ein berauschendes Farbenschauspiel.

The Garden of Dragons, a geological reserve located near the village of Gâlgău Almașului (Sălaj county).
Der Drachengarten (Grădina Zmeilor), ein geologisches Reservat auf dem Gebiet des Dorfes Gâlgău Almașului (Kreis Sălaj).

Local agricultural tourism services - a charming option for any one travelling to Romania.

Das agro-touristische Angebot der Ortschaften - eine verlockende Variante für diejenigen, die Rumänien bereisen.

The sanctuary at Sarmizegetusa Regia (Hunedoara county).
Das Heiligtum von Sarmizegetusa Regia (Kreis Hunedoara). ▷

Near the village of Moigrad (Sălaj county), the ruins of a major Daco-Roman settlement have been unearthed - *Porolissum.*
Auf dem Gebiet des Dorfes Moigrad (Kreis Sălaj) stieß man auf Spuren einer bedeutenden dazisch-römischen Niederlassung - Porolissum. ▷▷

The Forensis Basilica in the old Daco-Roman settlement of Adamclisi.
Die Basilica Forensis in der alten dazisch-römischen Niederlassung Adamclisi.

The geological and geomorphic reserve of Râpa Roșie, on the right slope of the Sebeș Valley.
Das geologische und geomorphologische Reservat Roter Berg (Râpa Roșie) am rechten Ufer des Sebeș-Flusses. ▷

The mud geysers of Buzău county - an oddity of nature.
Die Schlammvulkane im Kreis Buzău - ein seltsames Naturschauspiel.

An expanse of waters and land

2. Wasser und Erde so weit das Auge reicht

Many are the revelations of the murmuring Danube on its Romanian stretch: a spectacular gorge, 144 kilometres in length, along which can be found the majestic Cauldrons; banks along which has sprouted sub-Mediterranean vegetation (even though we are in a zone under continental climactic influence!); mysterious forms of karst relief; a delta which can truly named a paradise for plants and animals of all kinds; and the numerous vestiges of history...

There is a spirit of history that hovers over these vestiges, not allowing them to conceal their mysteries for all time. We should not forget the flourishing Greek colonies of the Black Sea coast, founded in the seventh and sixth centuries B.C.: Histria, Callatis (Mangalia), and Tomis (Constanța), the latter of which was sung in the *Tristia* and *Epistulae ex Ponto* of the Latin poet Ovid, exiled here by the Emperor Augustus in the first century A.D. Nor should we forget how the Roman legions crossed the Danube on their way to Dacia. The foot of the bridge built by Apollodoros of Damascus in 103-105 A.D. at the orders of the Emperor Trajan can still be found at Drobeta-Turnu Severin. Other vestiges from Roman times include the Herculanean Baths, ruined forts, and ancient roads, such as that built along the Danube, as attested by the *Tabula Traiana*, carved into the rock at the point where the Danube emerges from the Cauldrons. In the locality of Adamclisi, in the Dobrogea region, the ruins of the *Tropaeum Traiani* and the triumphal monument erected in honour of the Emperor Trajan's victory over the Dacians evoke the shadows of the past before our very eyes.

A journey down the Danube would not be complete without short stops at its wonderful ports: Orșova, Drobeta-Turnu Severin, Calafat, Turnu Măgurele, Giurgiu, Călarași, Cernavodă, Brăila, Galați, Tulcea, Sulina.

The Cauldrons.
Die "Donaukessel" (Cazanele Dunării).

Babacai - an enigmatic rock rises from the waters of the Danube.
Babacai - ein mysteriöser Felsblock mitten in der Donau. ▷

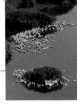
*A*uf dem Gebiet Rumäniens bietet die murmelnd dahinfließende Donau so manche Offenbarung: einen beeindruckenden Engpass in einer Gesamtlänge von 144 km, innerhalb dessen der majestätische Sektor der "Kessel" (Cazane) besonders auffällt; ferner die mediterrane Vegetation an den Ufern (obwohl wir uns in einem Gebiet befinden, das unter dem Einfluss des kontinentalen Klimas steht); interessante Karstformationen fallen ins Auge, und schließlich folgt das Donaudelta, das man zu Recht ein "Paradies" der Pflanzen und Tiere aller Art nennen kann und wo die Spuren der Vergangenheit zahllos sind.

Es herrscht hier ein Geist der Geschichte, der über den Zeugnissen alter Zeiten schwebt und nicht zulässt, dass diese in Vergessenheit geraten. Es wäre unverzeihlich zu vergessen, dass es einst am Ufer des Schwarzen Meeres blühende griechische Kolonien gegeben hat, die im 7.-6. Jahrhundert v.Chr. gegründet wurden: Histria, Callatis (Mangalia), Tomis (Constanța). Es wäre unverzeihlich zu vergessen, dass die römischen Truppen über die Donau setzten und ins Herz Daziens vordrangen. Ein Pfeiler der Brücke, die auf Befehl des Kaisers Trajan vom Architekten Apollodor von Damaskus in den Jahren 103-105 n.Chr. gebaut wurde, hat sich bei Drobeta-Turnu Severin bis heute erhalten. Andere Spuren aus jener Zeit finden wir in Herkulesbad (Băile Herculane) - die Thermen -, ferner Ruinen römischer Kastren, Spuren antiker Straßen, darunter die entlang der Donau, wie es die Inschrift der Tabula Traiana besagt, die auf Befehl des Kaisers da in den Fels geschlagen wurde, wo die Donau die "Kleinen Kessel" verlässt. In der Gemeinde Adamclisi in der Dobrudscha sind es die Ruinen der Festung Tropaeum Traiani und das zu Ehren des Sieges Kaiser Trajans über die Dazier errichtete Triumphdenkmal, die die Schatten der Vergangenheit wecken und uns vor Augen führen.

Eine Reise entlang der Donau wäre nicht komplett, würde man nicht auch in den schönen Hafenstädten Orșova, Drobeta-Turnu Severin, Calafat, Giurgiu, Călărași, Cernavodă, Brăila, Galați, Tulcea, Sulina kurz verweilen.

A snapshot from the world of crested pelicans, a protected species.
Schnappschuss aus der Welt der Krauskopfpelikane - eine unter Naturschutz stehende Art.

The Danube Delta is host to colonies of pelicans unique in Europe.
Das Donaudelta beherbergt in Europa einzigartige Pelikankolonien. ▷

In the Danube Delta, the largest wetland reserve in Europe (2,681 square kilometres), we find expanses of water and land teeming with primordial, luxuriant vegetation. We lose ourselves in groves of white willows or in mixed woods of poplar, oak, ash, elm, wild apple and pear. This is the domain of creeping plants, such as lianas and wild vines, which burgeon everywhere. The vast expanses of rushes and bulrushes create an unforgettable decor.

The waters stretch into the distance covered in wonderful carpets of white and yellow lily-pads, here and there broken by islands of floating vegetation. Everything here teems with life: the air hums to the flight of birds (pelicans, swans, egrets, white-tailed eagles); beneath the waters dart fishes (surgeon, sterlet, perch, pike, carp, crucian).

This exotic delta, between the river arms of the Chilia, Sulina and Sfântu Gheorghe, in which have been identified more than 1,200 species of plants and trees, 300 species of bird, and 100 species of fish, has been declared a UNESCO Biosphere Reserve.

Im Donaudelta, dem größten Feuchtgebiet-Reservat Europas (2681 qkm), finden wir riesige Wasserflächen und Land, auf dem es üppig grünt und blüht, wild wie am ersten Tag. Wir verirren uns in Auenwäldern von Weißweide oder aber in Mischwäldern, in denen Schwarzpappeln, Espen, Eichen, Eschen, Ulmen, Wildäpfel- und -birnbäume wachsen. Schlingpflanzen wie Lianen und wilder Wein wuchern und vernetzen alles. Riesige Flächen, mit Schilf, Rohr, Riedgras und Binsen bewachsen, bilden ein Dekor, das man so leicht nicht vergessen kann. So weit das Auge reicht, sind die Wasserflächen mit herrlichen Teppichen von weißen und gelben Seerosen bedeckt, ab und zu von schwimmenden Schilfinseln unterbrochen. Alles ist hier voller Leben: die Luft vibriert vom Flügelschlag der Vögel, die von überall auftauchen (Pelikane, Schwäne, Fuchsenten, Reiher, Löffler, Blässhühner, Weißkopfadler); unter der Wasseroberfläche sieht man die Fische herumschwimmen (Hausen, Stör, Sternhausen, Sterlet, Barsch, Hecht, Karpfen, Karausche). Dieses so exotische Delta, das zwischen den Flussarmen Chilia, Sulina und Sfântu Gheorghe liegt und in dem mehr als 1200 Pflanzen- und Baumarten, 300 Vogelarten, 100 Fischarten identifiziert wurden, ist seitens der UNESCO zu einem Biosphärenreservat erklärt worden.

Mating rituals of the spoonbill.
Paarungsspiele der Löffler.

Nest-building work in progress...
Die Beutelmeise "bei der Arbeit". ▷

Observed from up close and in silence, the lives of the cormorant and the night heron - some of the species of bird to be found in the Danube Delta - offer us many little surprises.

Aus der Nähe und in Ruhe betrachtet, bietet uns das Leben der Kormorane und Nachtreiher - Vogelarten, die im Donaudelta leben - kleine Überraschungen.

Romania has the rare privilege of having an opening onto the Black Sea, of approximately two hundred and forty kilometres. Along the southern Romanian coast, which stretches from the Midia Cape to Vama Veche, we can encounter both wild rocky shores and exotic beaches of fine sand. The hypnotically purling waves of the "Tranquil Sea" (the *Pontus Euxinus*, as it was known in antiquity) and the sunrises seen from its shores are an overwhelming, unforgettable experience.

In summer, the resorts of Mamaia, Năvodari, Eforie Nord, Eforie Sud, Olimp, Costinești, Neptun, Jupiter, Venus, Saturn and Mangalia teem with thousands of tourists here to enjoy the sun and beaches. Constanța, built on the ruins of a Greek colony (Tomis) from the seventh century B.C., owes its remarkable development to King Carol I, during whose reign the maritime port was modernised, by engineer Anghel Saligny. In this period, numerous hotels were also built, as well as the impressive Casino.

Rumänien erfreut sich des seltenen Vorteils, eine etwa 240 km lange Küste entlang des Schwarzen Meeres zu besitzen. In ihrem südlichen Teil, der vom Kap Midia bis Vama Veche reicht, trifft man sowohl auf wilde Felsküsten als auch auf exotische Strände mit feinstem Sand. Das hypnotische Rauschen der Wellen dieses "freundlichen Meeres" (Pontus Euxinus, wie es in der Antike genannt wurde), die Sonnenaufgänge, die man vom Ufer aus betrachten kann, sind geradezu berauschende Schauspiele, wie man sie so bald nicht vergisst. Wer sich weit aufs Meer hinauswagt, könnte mit ein wenig Glück die Spiele der freundlichen Delphine beobachten, die in diesem Meer leben.

Die Seebäder Mamaia, Năvodari, Eforie Nord, Eforie Sud, Olimp, Costineşti, Neptun, Jupiter, Venus, Saturn, Mangalia sind im Sommer von Tausenden Touristen bevölkert, die hierher kommen, um sich an der Sonne und dem Meereswasser zu erfreuen. Constanţa, auf den Ruinen einer griechischen Kolonie aus dem 7. Jahrhundert v. Chr. erbaut, verdankt seinen bemerkenswerten Aufstieg König Carol I., während dessen Regierungszeit man den Seehafen modernisierte, eine Arbeit, die unter Leitung des Ingenieurs Anghel Saligny durchgeführt wurde. Zur selben Zeit entstanden auch zahlreiche Hotels und das schmucke Kasino.

Vast plains, oceans of green, yellow and red hues, stretch to the limitless horizon...

Riesige Fluren gleich Meeren in grünen, gelben, roten Farbtönen gehen in die Grenzenlosigkeit des Horizonts über.

The Danube carries us onwards, deeper into Romania...
Und die Donau trägt uns weiter, anderen Zielen in Rumänien entgegen . . .

Villages, people, traditions and faith

3. Dörfer, Menschen, Traditionen und Glauben

You have not seen Romania until you visit its villages, with their picturesque, archaic atmosphere, which is paradoxically not at all anachronistic, given that everything throbs with life. You will be able to feast your ears on the ballads, *doinas* (traditional songs) and carols, and your eyes on the colourful peasant rugs, which are woven on the loom at home and used as carpets or to decorate the walls. Only then will you be able to understand the depths of the folk spirit. You would also do well to visit the potters' workshops at Horezu (Vâlcea County), Marginea and Rădăuți (Suceava County), Vama (Satu Mare County), which religiously preserve the secrets of ancient techniques for making ceramic vases, decorated with folk motifs of exquisite taste. Then you should observe the amazing metamorphoses of wood: in Bukowina, Maramureș or the Apuseni Mountains, there flourishes a veritable culture of woodworking, and the meticulously carved porches of churches and houses are like jewels.

The traditions and customs of the Romanians have a rarely encountered savour. The people hereabouts are closely attached to their customs. At a time when city folk are homogenising everything and forgetting the essence of the things amongst which they dwell, the Romanian peasant refuses to give up his beliefs and stubbornly preserves the last remnants of his ancestral pastoral culture. In the mountains and hills of certain areas of Romania - especially the Sibiu area and the Rucăr-Bran corridor - you may still meet shepherds who know the ancient methods of making cheese, cottage cheese and "bulz" (a dish of cheese and polenta). Every year, there are dozens of festivals all over Romania which revive rituals whose real meanings have been partially forgotten but which nevertheless still preserve the essential. For example, the Maidens' Market at Muntele Găina, an ancient pastoral festival, has already won over all Romanians. Every year, on the Sunday before Saint Elijah's Day (20 July), thousands of people from all over the country repeat the sacred ritual of making the ascent to the glade situated at the top of the mountain, at a height of 1,467 metres.

It is not possible to speak of the Romanian Christmas and New Year festivities without mentioning the alluring aroma of "cozonac" (a traditional cake), the carols, the rituals connected to the cutting of the pig, and the shouts of the bands of masked revellers, dressed as bears, who roam the villages wishing householders a plentiful year. At Easter, Romanians prepare "pasca" (a kind of cheesecake) and masterfully decorate eggs: each one of these eggs, painstakingly painted with dozens of traditional motifs, in the predominant colours of red, yellow and black, may be regarded as a miniature work of art.

In the villages still persists the belief in a "magical world" dominated by supernatural forces, inhabited by demons, pixies, fairies, ghosts and witches. Romanian superstitions recreate an archaic universe, in which each element is redolent with meaning. Peasants still know how to weave wonderful tales, and everyday talk is still coloured by countless wise sayings reminiscent of the sagacity of the Orient.

The world beyond is a living presence for these peasants. They know how to honour their dead, with certain festivals being exclusively dedicated to the remembrance of departed souls. On the Day of the Dead, which is celebrated each autumn, thousands of candles are lit by the faithful and gleam in the cemeteries until the dawn of the next day.

◁◁ Wedding procession in Țara Oașului.
Hochzeitszug im Oașer Land.

Swain wearing a "clop" adorned with a peacock feather, Năsăud region.
Jüngling mit traditionellem Hut (clop) mit Pfauenfederschmuck aus dem Năsăud-Gebiet.

*F*alls Sie Rumänien besucht und nicht auch in den Dörfern mit ihrer malerischen archaischen Atmosphäre geweilt haben, die gar nicht anachronisch wirkt, da hier das Leben in vollen Zügen pulst, haben Sie noch nicht alles gesehen. Falls Sie Rumänien besucht und nicht auch einen gemütlichen Plausch mit seinen Menschen geführt haben, für welche das Einhalten der Traditionen selbstverständlich ist, haben Sie den Zauber des Landes noch nicht entdeckt. Lassen Sie Ihre Ohren erfreuen von den Doinen und Balladen (traditionelle Gesänge) und Weihnachtsliedern, und Ihre Augen vom Anblick der rumänischen Wandbehänge und Teppiche, die die Bäuerinnen selbst im Haus am Webstuhl aus Wolle fertigen. Sie werden entweder auf den Fußboden gelegt oder sie zieren die Wände. Erst danach werden Sie die Tiefe des Volksgenius verstehen. Besuchen Sie unbedingt die Werkstätten der Töpfer in Horezu (Kreis Vâlcea), in Marginea und Rădăuți (Kreis Suceava), in Vama (Kreis Satu Mare), die die Geheimnisse der uralten Techniken zur Herstellung der Keramikgefäße heilig halten. Das Dekor dieser Volkskeramik ist immer von vollendetem Geschmack. Auch die erstaunliche Metamorphose des Holzes müssen Sie verfolgen. In der Maramureș, der Bukowina oder in den Westkarpaten, wo geradezu eine Zivilisation des Holzes aufgeblüht ist, gleichen die schönen Häuser mit ihren offenen Vorlauben und die Kirchen mit ihrem minuziös ausgeführten Schnitzwerk wahren Schmuckstücken.

Die Traditionen und Sitten der Rumänen haben etwas ganz Besonderes an sich. Die Menschen halten große Stücke auf ihre Bräuche. Im Berg- und Hügelland gewisser Zonen in Rumänien - vor allem in der Gegend von Hermannstadt (Sibiu) oder im Durchbruch Rucăr-Bran - kann man immer wieder die Schafherden mit ihren Hirten antreffen, die die alten Techniken der Milchverarbeitung zu Käse, Süßkäse, Hüttenkäse und der Hirtenspeise "bulz" (mit Käse gefüllte Maisbreiklöße) noch bestens kennen. Jahr für Jahr werden in allen Regionen Rumäniens an zahlreichen Feiertagen Rituale wieder belebt, deren wahrer Sinn zum Teil schon verloren ging, doch der festliche Geist blieb erhalten. Alle diese Bräuche stehen mit dem Leben der Hirten, mit ihrer Tätigkeit im Laufe des Jahres in enger Verbindung.

Von den rumänischen Festlichkeiten anlässlich der Weihnachtsfeiertage und des Neujahrs können wir nicht sprechen, ohne den verlockenden Duft des Backwerks zu erwähnen, die Lieder und Zurufe der Maskierten (Bären, Ziegen, Pferdchen), die durch die Dörfer ziehen und den Hauswirten ein gesegnetes Jahr wünschen; auch die Rituale im Zusammenhang mit dem Schweineschlachten und der Verarbeitung des Fleisches sind erwähnenswert. Zu Ostern backen die rumänischen Frauen einen speziellen Osterkuchen, "pască" genannt, und verzieren die Eier mit viel Geschick. Jedes einzelne dieser peinlich genau dekorierten Eier weist Dutzende von traditionellen Mustern und ein paar vorherrschende Farben (rot, gelb, schwarz) auf und könnte ein kleines Kunstwerk genannt werden.

In den Dörfern glaubt man noch an die "magische Welt", die von überirdischen Kräften gelenkt und von Dämonen, Elfen, Feen, Gespenstern und Zauberinnen bevölkert wird. Der Aberglaube der Rumänen lässt eine archaische Weltanschauung erkennen, in der jedes Element seine Bedeutung hat. Die Bauern verstehen es meisterhaft, Schwänke zu erzählen, ihre Sprache ist immer bilderreich, und die vielen geistreichen Aussprüche, die ihre Alltagssprache würzen, erinnern irgendwie an die Weisheiten des Orients.

Scenes from the world of the Romanian village: fairytale houses, picturesque customs, traditional crafts, serene people. *Blick in die Welt der rumänischen Dörfer: Häuser wie im Märchen, malerische Bräuche, traditionelle Handwerke, heitere Menschen.*

At Easter, delicious "*cozonac*", "*pască*" and painted eggs are always to found on the Romanian festive table.

Am Ostertag dürfen vom Tisch der Rumänen keineswegs die bunten Eier, Hefegebäck und der traditionelle Osterkuchen "pască" fehlen. ▷▷

The unaffected way in which children wear traditional costume is a striking feature of Romania.

Ein weiterer erstaunlicher Anblick in Rumänien: die Selbstverständlichkeit, mit der die Kinder Tracht und Bräuche der Eltern übernehmen.

The everyday life of young people in Romania does not seem much different from that of their western counterparts. They have the same musical tastes, they wear the same fashions, and they are up to date with all the latest technology. On festive days, however, they rediscover the picturesque beauty of their ancestral traditions.

Im alltäglichen Leben scheinen sich die jungen Leute aus Rumänien nicht von denen des Westens zu unterscheiden. Sie bevorzugen die gleiche Musik, kleiden sich nach neuester Mode, kennen die neuesten Entdeckungen auf dem Gebiet der Technik. An Feiertagen jedoch entdecken sie wieder die malerische Schönheit der Bräuche ihrer Ahnen.

The life of the Romanians seems always to have been dominated by a profound sense of the religious. It might be said that Romania, which is pre-eminently Orthodox, is a land of churches, hermitages and monasteries. The life of the people in each settlement in these regions centres around a church, which is regarded as the *axis mundi*. Sheltered from the stress and bustle of our everyday life, the hermitages and monasteries of Romania, whence have withdrawn monks in search of *hesykhia* (or spiritual tranquillity), leading lives of prayer and fasting, are wonderful places in which to reflect and to rediscover God.

Das Leben der Rumänen war anscheinend seit je her von einem tief religiösen Gefühl durchdrungen. Man kann sagen, dass Rumänien - ein vorwiegend orthodoxes Gebiet - ein Land der Kirchen, Einsiedeleien und Klöster ist. Das Leben der Menschen einer jeden Niederlassung in diesem Land ist auf die Kirche ausgerichtet, sie ist der Mittelpunkt ihres Lebens. Die Einsiedeleien und Klöster liegen abseits des Alltagsgewirrs und der Unruhe unserer Tage. Hier, wohin sich die Mönche zurückzogen, um fern dem lärmenden Alltag in Einsamkeit ein Leben mit Fasten und Beten zu führen, gibt es herrliche Plätzchen, wo man in sich gehen und Gott wieder finden kann.

The Aluniş Cave and the Cave of Dionisie Torcătorul (Buzău county) - places of prayer for the hermits of Wallachia in days of old.
Die Grotte von Aluniş und die Grotte des Dionisie Torcătorul (Kreis Buzău) - alte Gebetsstätten der Einsiedler aus der Walachei.

The historical Romanian province of Moldavia is celebrated throughout the world for its splendid churches and monasteries, founded by god-fearing Moldavian boyars (Voroneț, Putna, Humor, Sucevița, Moldovița, Arbore, Bogdana, Pătrăuți, Bălinești, Probota, Dragomirna). The beauty of the frescoes, painted in inimitable hues of blue, red, yellow and green, which adorn the exterior walls of some monasteries, is overwhelming; these ancient images, which recount the sacred and profane history of the world, are unforgettable.

Die historische rumänische Provinz Moldau ist in aller Welt wegen ihrer wunderbaren Kirchen und Klöster berühmt, die von gottesfürchtigen moldauischen Herrschern und Bojaren gestiftet wurden (Voroneț, Putna, Humor, Sucevița, Moldovița, Arbore, Bogdana, Pătrăuți, Probota, Dragomirna). Die Schönheit der Fresken, die in unverwechselbaren blauen, roten, gelben und grünen Farbtönen ausgeführt sind und die Außenwände einiger Klosterkirchen bedecken, ist geradezu überwältigend. Nachdem man diese alten Bilder gesehen hat, die die heilige und profane Geschichte der Welt wieder aufleben lassen, ist es unmöglich, sie jemals wieder zu vergessen.

The cupola of the church at Moldovița, the monastery founded by Petru Rareș in 1532.
Das Deckengewölbe der 1532 von Petru Rareș gestifteten Klosterkirche Moldovița.

The blue of the exterior murals on the church of the Voroneț Monastery, built by Stephen the Great in 1488, has long been famous... The murals were painted during the reign of Petru Rareș, between 1534 and 1535.
Das Blau der Außenfresken der Klosterkirche Voroneț, 1488 vom Herrscher Stefan dem Großen (Ștefan cel Mare) gestiftet, ist berühmt... Die Malereien wurden zur Zeit von Petru Rareș (1534-1535) ausgeführt. ▷

Compared with the massive stone churches, small wooden churches provide a different order of spatiality. Nowhere is it more fitting than in Maramureș to experience the full splendour achieved by the art of woodworking in Romania. Impressive examples of peasant art and expressions of rural spirituality, the wooden churches of Maramureș, with their tapering spires reaching to the heavens, seem to have overcome the essentially perishable nature of the material from which they were fashioned.

Im Vergleich zu den massiven Kirchen aus Stein ist der Innenraum der kleinen Holzkirchen anders eingeteilt. Um den hohen Grad zu veranschaulichen, den die Kunst der Holzbauten in Rumänien erreicht hat, ist die Maramureș wohl der geeignetste Ort. Die Holzkirchen von hier mit ihren schlanken Türmen, die gleichsam den Himmel zu erreichen suchen, sind bewundernswerte Beispiele der bäuerlichen Kunst, ein Ausdruck der dörflichen Spiritualität. Man hat den Eindruck, dass sie die Vergänglichkeit des Elements, aus dem sie gebaut wurden, überwunden haben.

What immediately attracts our attention when we travel through Romania is the large number of churches, to be found at every step. Most of them are over a hundred years old. We naturally wonder as to what it might mean. Why did the people of these parts feel the need to build so many places of worship, these veritable architectural wonders, so beautifully decorated and richly endowed? The old folk will answer simply: so that God might help them in all their affairs.

Was uns bei einer Reise durch Rumänien besonders auffällt, ist die große Anzahl von Gotteshäusern, die man so gut wie überall antrifft. Die meisten sind Hunderte Jahre alt. Was hat das zu bedeuten? fragen wir uns zu Recht. Warum haben die hier lebenden Menschen das Bedürfnis empfunden, so viele Kultbauten zu errichten, wahre architektonische Wunderwerke, schön ausgeschmückt und mit Schenkungen reich bedacht? Die hier ansässigen Alten hätten gleich eine einfache Antwort parat: "Damit Gott ihnen in allem hilft, was sie sich vornehmen."

The old churches of Wallachia: Cozia Monastery (1387-1388), Curtea de Argeș Monastery (1512-1517), Hurez Monastery (1697).
Alte Kultstätten der Walachei : das Kloster Cozia (1387-1388), das Kloster Curtea de Argeș (1512-1517), das Kloster Hurez (1697).

At the centre of the rural settlements founded by Saxon colonists in the Romanian province of Transylvania in the twelfth century there stand fortified churches, which once served as places of refuge in times of danger. Many of these fortress-like stronghold churches, built mainly after the Tartar invasion of 1241, have been preserved.

Im Zentrum der alten Dörfer, die von den deutschen Kolonisten - den Siebenbürger Sachsen - in der rumänischen Provinz Transsilvanien im 12. Jahrhundert gegründet wurden, steht die Kirchenburg, die im Falle einer Gefahr auch als Zufluchtsort diente. Heute noch stehen viele dieser Wehrkirchen, die wie kleine Burgen aussehen; die meisten von ihnen entstanden nach dem Tatareneinfall im Jahr 1241.

An Evangelical church, built in the Gothic style, has been preserved in the middle of the peasant citadel at Viscri (thirteenth-sixteenth century).
Inmitten der Bauernburg von Weißkirch (Viscri) - 13.-16. Jahrhundert - hat sich eine alte evangelische Kirche in gotischem Stil erhalten. ▷

The fortified church at Cincu village, built in the thirteenth century, preserves a priceless polyptic altar, painted by Vincentius of Sibiu in 1521.
Die Kirchenburg des Dorfes Großschenk (Cincu), im 13. Jahrhundert erbaut, hat einen wertvollen Flügelaltar, den der Künstler Vincentius aus Hermannstadt (Sibiu) 1521 mit Malereien versah.

The thirteenth century fortified church within the citadel of Merghindeal (Sibiu county).
Die Kirchenburg von Mergeln (Merghindeal) - Kreis Sibiu - aus dem 13. Jahrhundert.

Romania: images from a world of religious faith.
Rumänien – Ausschnitt aus einer Welt des Glaubens.

Cityscapes

4. Stadtansichten

The blend of old and new that can be met in Romanian towns is sometimes disconcerting. Constructions of concrete and steel and streets full of the dizzying din so characteristic of our times are to be found alongside piazzas flanked by magnificent edifices in the Baroque, Renaissance, Secession or Neo-classical styles, as well as quiet streets shaded by chestnut trees... Here and there can be discovered the scars left by the communist regime, beneath whose nefarious rule Romania endured for almost half a century. Thousands of old houses were demolished in Romanian towns during that period, to make way for homogenous, ugly apartment blocks. Since the Revolution of 1989, which led to the overthrow of dictator Nicolae Ceaușescu and the istallation of democracy, a market economy has been established. Since then, building work has gone on at fever pitch seemingly everywhere, resulting in a spectacular and rapid transformation in the appearance of the old cities. The urban trend now represents a shift away from the centre and a valorisation of the outskirts.

Bucharest, the capital of Romania, is a genuine European city, with magnificent buildings: the National Savings Bank, the National Museum of History, the Military Club, the National Museum of Art (formerly the Royal Palace), the Central University Library (formerly the Palace of the Carol I University Foundation), the Romanian Athenaeum, the George Enescu Museum (the Cantacuzino Palace), the Municipality of Bucharest Museum of History (the Șuțu Palace). In former times, Bucharest was known as the "Little Paris". Today, the dynamic life of this fascinating metropolis, in step with the times, manifests a different kind of charm, which we invite you to discover for yourselves.

The Hill of the Metropolis, on which are sited the Church of the Patriarchate, founded in 1656-1658 by Prince Constantin Șerban Basarab, the bell tower, built by Constantin Brâncoveanu in 1698, and the Palace of the Patriarchate.
Der Metropoliehügel, auf dem sich die Patriarchiekirche erhebt, 1656-1658 vom Herrscher Constantin Șerban Basarab gestiftet, ferner der 1698 von Constantin Brâncoveanu erbaute Glockenturm sowie das Patriarchiepalais.

The Romanian Athenaeum (1886-1888), with its neoclassical facade and baroque cupola.
Das Rumänische Athenäum (1886-1888) mit neoklassischer Fassade und einer Barockkuppel. ▷

*D*as Zusammentreffen von Neu und Alt, das uns in den rumänischen Städten begegnet, wirkt manchmal verwirrend. Die Bauten aus Beton und Glas, die Straßen voller betäubendem Gesumme, daneben Plätze, an denen bemerkenswerte Gebäude stehen, die von verschiedenen Stilarten geprägt sind, und einsame Straßen, in denen Kastanienbäume Schatten spenden. Hie und da trifft man auf Spuren des kommunistischen Regimes, unter dessen unheilvollem Zeichen Rumänien fast ein halbes Jahrhundert lang gestanden hat. Tausende alter Häuser wurden damals in den rumänischen Städten abgetragen, um Platz zu schaffen für unästhetische Einheitsbauten (Wohnblocks). Nach der Revolution von 1989, die zum Fall des Diktators Nicolae Ceaușescu und zur Einsetzung der Demokratie führte, haben sich in Rumänien die Gesetze der Marktwirtschaft durchgesetzt. Seither ist fast überall das Baufieber ausgebrochen, was eine spektakuläre und rapide Veränderung im Aussehen der großen Städte zur Folge hatte.

Bukarest, die Hauptstadt Rumäniens, ist eine europäische Stadt, die sich durch ihre glanzvollen Bauten auszeichnet: die Spar- und Depositenkasse, das Nationalmuseum für Geschichte, das Militärkasino, das Nationalmuseum für Kunst (der ehemalige Königspalast), die Zentrale Universitätsbibliothek (das einstige Palais der Universitätsstiftung Carol I.), das Rumänische Athenäum, das Museum George Enescu (im Palais Cantacuzino), das Museum für Geschichte des Munizipiums Bukarest (im Palais Șuțu). Einst wurde das elegante Bukarest "Klein-Paris" genannt. Nun strahlt das dynamische Leben dieser faszinierenden Metropole den heutigen Zeiten entsprechend einen andersartigen Zauber aus, wir laden Sie ein, diesen selbst zu entdecken.

The Linden Inn: a shopping arcade built in 1833 and situated between Lipscani and Blănari streets in the historic centre of Bucharest.
Die Kunstgalerie Hanul cu Tei (Lindenherberge), ehemals ein 1833 erbauter Handelshof zwischen der Lipscani- und der Blănari-Straße im historischen Teil von Bukarest.

The fountain at the centre of Luigi Cazzavillan Park, near Casa Radio.
Der Denkmal-Brunnen im Park Luigi Cazzavillan in der Nähe des Rundfunkhauses. ▷

The National Savings Bank Palace, built between 1896 and 1900 according to the plans of French architect Paul Gottereau.

Der Palast der Spar- und Depositenbank (CEC) ist 1896-1900 nach den Plänen des französischen Architekten Paul Gottereau erbaut worden.

The Macca-Villacrosse Passage, opened in 1891, links Calea Victoriei and Eugeniu Carada Street.

Die Passage Macca-Villacrosse, 1891 eingeweiht, verbindet die Calea Victoriei mit der Eugeniu-Carada-Straße. ▷

Victory Plaza: the modern face of Bucharest.
Das moderne Antlitz von Bukarest.

University Plaza: night view.
Der Universitätsplatz – Nachtaufnahme. ▷

The twelfth century Saxon colonists in Transylvania developed a typically Germanic structure in this area. *Sighișoara*, the only inhabited mediaeval citadel in Southeast Europe, was declared a World Heritage Site by UNESCO in 1999. *Sibiu*, a modern, western city, still preserves traces of the flourishing mediaeval burg of former times, as well as buildings specific to the Viennese Baroque, built during the time of the Hapsburg Empire. *Cluj-Napoca* is one of Romania's major centres of culture and learning. There are nine institutes of higher learning here, with forty-nine faculties, and numerous research institutions.

The old centre of *Baia Mare*, situated at the foot of the Gutâi Mountains, is dominated by Stephen's Tower, surrounded by numerous recently restored baroque edifices. Visitors to *Satu Mare* are ravished by the architectural diversity of the city, where they can admire the baroque Reformed Church, the neo-classical Roman Catholic cathedral, the baroque and neo-Gothic Vácsay House, and the Secession White House. *Brașov*, sited at the foot of the Tâmpa Mountain, is one of the most celebrated tourist centres in the country. Near the city can be found numerous remains of Saxon fortifications. In the city of *Alba Iulia,* the Act of Union between Romania and the provinces of Transylvania, Banat, Maramureș and Crișana was signed on 1 December 1918.

The Banat is synonymous with *Timișoara*, the city on the Bega River. Timisoara bears the most visible imprint of the Baroque: the old City Hall, the Palace of the Prefecture, the Roman Catholic Episcopal Palace, the St Catherine Roman Catholic Church etc. In *Arad*, you can visit a citadel dating from the sixteenth century, the Red Church, the Orthodox Cathedral, the Roman Catholic Church, the Serbian Church and the Palace of Culture.

The cities of Moldavia are bathed in a milder, more serene atmosphere. Here, time seems to move more slowly. This harmony is perhaps due to the dozens of monasteries founded in the immediate vicinity of the cities. In Moldavia, you will find settlements large (cities such as *Suceava, Bacău, Galați, Piatra-Neamț*) and small (market towns like *Vaslui, Focșani, Târgu Neamț*). The ineffably charming city of *Iași*, which, like Rome, is sited on seven hills, is without doubt the heart of Moldavia.

Romania's numerous spas (*Băile Herculane, Sovata, Băile Felix, Slănic Moldova, Băile Olănești, Călimănești-Căciulata, Borsec, Tușnad*) and mountain resorts (*Poiana Brașov, Sinaia, Bușteni, Predeal, Durău, Semenic, Muntele Mic*) recommend it as an ideal place to spend your holidays.

Dobrogea is one of the most picturesque of the Romanian regions: the Black Sea coast, with the resorts of *Mamaia, Eforie, Neptun, Costinești, Saturn, Venus* and *Jupiter* is invaded by thousands of tourists in the summer. In *Constanța* (the ancient Greek colony of Tomis), a Black Sea port, the Genoese built a lighthouse in the thirteenth century, which is preserved to the present day. Over the settlements of Dobrogea still hovers the perfume of the Levant, reminding us of the times when the region was part of the Ottoman Empire (1417-1878).

The cities of Romania, large or small, old or new, constantly show that every place has its own way of surprising the traveller.

Peleș Castle at Sinaia, the former residence of the kings of Romania.
Schloss Peleș in Sinaia, ehemalige Sommerresidenz der Könige Rumäniens.

*D*ie Siebenbürger Sachsen, die im 12. Jahrhundert in Transsilvanien angesiedelt wurden, haben in diesem Raum Niederlassungen gegründet, die eine typisch deutsche Struktur aufwiesen. Schäßburg (Sighişoara), die einzige bewohnte Burg Südosteuropas, wurde 1999 seitens der UNESCO zu einem Weltkulturerbe erklärt. Hermannstadt (Sibiu), eine moderne, westliche Stadt, bewahrt heute noch Spuren der einstigen blühenden mittelalterlichen Stadt und umfasst Bauten mit Architekturelementen, die für den Wiener Barock spezifisch sind und zur Zeit der habsburgischen Verwaltung entstanden. Klausenburg (Cluj-Napoca) ist ein bedeutendes kulturell-wissenschaftliches und Unterrichtszentrum Rumäniens. Hier gibt es 9 Hochschulen mit 49 Fakultäten und zahlreiche Forschungsinstitute. Das alte Zentrum von Baia Mare, der Stadt am Fuße der Gutâi-Berge, wird vom Stefansdom beherrscht. Rundum erheben sich zahlreiche, kürzlich renovierte Barockbauten. Wer Sathmar (Satu Mare) besucht hat, bleibt von der architektonischen Vielfalt der Stadt beeindruckt. Hier kann man u.a. die reformierte Kirche (die Kirche mit Ketten) im Barockstil, die römisch-katholische Kathedrale und das Bischofspalais in neuklassischem Stil, das Vácsay-Haus im Barock- und neugotischen Stil, das Weiße Haus im Sezessionsstil bewundern. Kronstadt (Braşov), am Fuße der Zinne (Tâmpa) gelegen, ist eines der größten Touristikzentren des Landes. In seiner Umgebung haben sich die Ruinen zahlreicher sächsischer Befestigungen erhalten. In Alba Iulia ist am 1.Dezember 1918 der Akt der Vereinigung Transsilvaniens, des Banats, der Maramureş und des Kreischlandes mit Rumänien unterzeichnet worden.

Banat heißt Temesvar (Timişoara), die Stadt an der Bega, die Stadt, die hauptsächlich von Barockbauten geprägt ist (das alte Rathaus, das Palais der Präfektur, das römisch-katholische Bischofspalais, die römisch-katholische Kirche zur heiligen Katharina u.a.). In Arad können Sie eine Burg aus dem 16. Jahrhundert besichtigen, ferner die Rote Kirche, die orthodoxe Kathedrale, die römisch-katholische Kirche, die serbische Kirche, das Kulturpalais.

Die moldauischen Städte sind in eine sanftere, heitere Atmosphäre gehüllt. Hier scheint die Zeit noch Geduld zu haben. Diese Harmonie ist wohl auch den vielen Klöstern in nächster Nähe der Städte zu verdanken. Sie werden in der Moldau sowohl größere Städte antreffen (Suceava, Bacău, Galaţi, Piatra-Neamţ) als auch kleinere, die eher wie Marktflecken aussehen (Vaslui, Focşani, Tàrgu-Neamţ). Jassy (Iaşi), die Stadt auf sieben Hügeln wie Rom, ist selbstverständlich das Herz der Moldau. Ein Spaziergang durch Jassy gereicht unweigerlich zu einem großen Vergnügen.

Unzählige Bade- und Luftkurorte (Herkulesbad, Sovata, Felixbad, Slănic Moldova, Olăneşti, Călimăneşti-Căciulata, Borsec, Tuşnad) und Gebirgskurorte (Schulerau-Poiana Braşov, Sinaia, Buşteni, Predeal, Durău, Semenic, Muntele Mic) sind Grund genug, Rumänien als idealen Ferienort zu enmpfehlen.

Die Dobrudscha ist eine der malerischsten Gegenden Rumäniens: die Schwarzmeerküste mit den Seebädern Mamaia, Eforie, Neptun, Costineşti, Saturn, Venus, Jupiter ist im Sommer von Tausenden Touristen überlaufen. In Constanţa (der antiken griechischen Kolonie Tomis), der Hafenstadt am Schwarzen Meer, haben die Genueser im 13. Jahrhundert einen Leuchtturm gebaut, der heute noch steht. Über den Ortschaften der Dobrudscha schwebt noch immer ein levantinisches Aroma, das uns an die Zeiten erinnert, da dieses Gebiet von den Türken beherrscht wurde (1417-1878).

Die rumänischen Städte, größere oder kleinere, ältere oder neuere, beweisen uns immer wieder das Gleiche: Jeder Ort überrascht den Reisenden in seiner Art.

The John the Baptist Cathedral in Ploieşti, with its sixty metre high steeple.
Die Kathedrale des Heiligen Johannes des Täufers (Sfântul Ioan Botezătorul) aus Ploieşti mit ihrem 60 m hohen Turm.

The Church of the Dormition of the Mother of God, in Council Square in Brașov.
Die Kirche Mariä Himmelfahrt (Adormirea Maicii Domnului) am Rathausplatz in Kronstadt (Brașov). ▷

The ruins of the princely court at Târgoviște (the former capital of Wallachia), constructed successively by Mircea the Old, Petru Cercel, Matei Basarab, Radu the Great, and Constantin Brâncoveanu.

Die Ruinen des Fürstenhofes in Târgoviște (ehemaliger Herrschersitz der Walachei). An diesem haben der Reihe nach die Fürsten Mircea der Alte (cel Batrân), Petru Cercel, Matei Basarab, Radu der Große (cel Mare) und Constantin Brâncoveanu bauen lassen.

Sibiu, a mediaeval burg first attested in 1191, has been designated by the Council of Europe as "European Capital of Culture" in 2007.

Hermannstadt (Sibiu), eine Stadt aus dem Mittelalter, 1191 erstmals urkundlich erwähnt, wurde vom Europarat zur "Europäischen Kulturhauptstadt des Jahres 2007 gekürt. ▷

The baroque Palace of the Prefecture and the Secession-style Palace of Culture in Târgu Mureș.
Der Palast der Präfektur im Barockstil und das Kulturpalais im Sezessionsstil in Târgu Mureș.

The historic centre of Alba Iulia is dominated by two imposing edifices: the Orthodox Cathedral of the Holy Trinity and the Roman Catholic Cathedral of Saint Michael.

Das Zentrum der Stadt Alba Iulia wird von zwei beeindruckenden Bauten beherrscht: der orthodoxen Kathedrale zur Heiligen Dreieinigkeit und der römisch-katholischen Kirche zum Heiligen Michael. ▷▷

Sighișoara, the only inhabited citadel in south-east Europe, has been designated a World Heritage Site by UNESCO.

Schässburg (Sighișoara), die einzige bewohnte Burg Südosteuropas, wurde ins UNESCO-Weltkulturerbe aufgenommen.

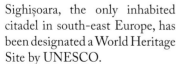

The Roman Catholic Cathedral of Saint Michael in Cluj-Napoca, built between 1349 and 1450.
Die römisch-katholische Kathedrale zum Heiligen Michael in Klausenburg (Cluj-Napoca), zwischen 1349 und 1450 erbaut. ▷

The Hotel Dacia in Satu Mare, built in the Secession style in 1902.
Das Hotel Dacia in Sathmar, im Jahre 1902 im Sezessionsstil erbaut.

The Tower of Stephen (fifteenth century) in Baia Mare.
Der Stefansturm (15. Jh.) in Baia Mare.

The eclectic Palace of Culture (1910-1913) in Arad. ▷
Das Kulturpalais von Arad (1910–1913) in eklektischem Stil.

The Orthodox cathedral of the Three Holy Hierarchs (1936-1946) in Timișoara, the city that "set the tone" for the 1989 Revolution, in which the communist regime was deposed.
Die orthodoxe Kathedrale Die drei heiligen Erzväter (Sfinții Trei Ierarhi; 1936-1946) aus Temesvar (Timișoara), der Stadt, wo im Dezember 1989 die Revolution ihren Anfang nahm, in deren Folge das kommunistische Regime gestürzt wurde. ▷▷

Oradea, the city on the Crișu Repede River.
Großwardein (Oradea), die Stadt an der Schnellen Kreisch.

Craiova: the building of the Administrative Palace (today the Prefecture), built between 1912 and 1913, according to the plans of architect Petre Antonescu.

Craiova: Das Gebäude des Verwaltungspalastes (heute Präfektur), 1912-1913 nach Plänen des Architekten Petre Antonescu erbaut. ▷

Drobeta-Turnu Severin: the statue representing Decebal, the legendary king of the Dacians between 87 and 106 A.D.

Drobeta-Turnu Severin: die Statue Dezebals, des sagenumwobenen Königs der Dazier (87-106 u.Z.).

Pitești: the Museum of Argeș county.
Das Kreismuseum aus Pitești.

After Suceava became capital of Moldavia, in 1388, Prince Petru I Muşat built a citadel in the south-east quarter of the city, which was later extended by Stephen the Great.

Nachdem Suceava 1388 Hauptstadt der Moldau geworden war, baute der Fürst Petru I. Muşat im Südosten der Stadt eine Burg, die Stefan der Große später noch weiter ausbaute. ▷

The neo-Gothic edifice of the Palace of Culture (1907-1926) in Jassy (Iaşi), built on the site of the former courts, today houses an extensive museum complex.

Der neugotische Bau des Kulturpalastes von Jassy (Iaşi) (1907-1926) erhebt sich da, wo einst der Fürstenhof stand, und beherbergt heute einen großen musealen Komplex.

Aerial view over the shoreline of the maritime port of Constanța, dominated by the elegant silhouette of the Art Nouveau style Casino, built between 1907 and 1910.

Luftbild von der Küstenpromenade des Touristenhafens von Constanța, die von der eleganten Silhouette des 1907-1910 im Jugendstil erbauten Kasinos beherrscht wird. ▷

Tulcea - gateway to the Danube Delta.
Tulcea – das "Eingangstor zum Donaudelta".

Our journey through Romania ends here... Behind us we leave beautiful moments, which will transform into memories, illumining our thoughts like the glimmer of a lighthouse.
Hier beenden wir unsere Reise durch Rumänien . . . Diese wunderschönen Augenblicke werden zurückbleiben, sich in Erinnerungen verwandeln und unsere Gedanken erhellen wie das funkelnde Aufleuchten eines Leuchtturms des Nachts. ▷▷